ALL MY THOUGHTS

TARQUIN

for the dreamers
and the lonely
for the broken
and the lost
all my thoughts
and all my love

Tarquin
xx

ALL MY HEARTACHE

I was addicted to you,

the way the sea is addicted to the shore.

How can I let go of these cravings

even when you aren't there

anymore?

You left me colorless

chasing after dreams

that no longer included you

now my heart aches so badly in my chest

and I don't know what to do.

Sometimes
I think you only came into my life
to break my heart.

But the most tragic thing was not that you left.

It was that in all the heartache, I'd forgotten

who I was. I'd stopped caring about what I

wanted or needed. While you stopped fighting

for us, I'd stopped fighting for me.

I still don't know how you so easily moved on
and I'm still here, missing the way you laughed,
and the sunlight in your eyes, missing the way
you held coffee mugs, and the touch of your
skin on mine. How does the sound of your name
still make my lips tremble and my heart ache,
even after all this time?

I'm such a mess,
but I thought I was
the mess you wanted.

Do you know what this feels like, to hold back tears because boys don't cry.

Do you know what this feels like to be alone, to hide, to always say I'm fine and lie.

Do you know what this feels like to miss her so badly it hurts, to have such a broken heart, it feels like you're cursed.

I have two longings,
one to let you go
and the other for
you to come home.

But I don't know how to live in this world

without you. I'm struggling to re learn every

step without you by my side. I felt your love like

I felt the world at my feet and now I will feel the

grief like I feel the world on my shoulders.

You asked me if you were hard to love and I

tried to convince you that everything I needed

was with you. But in the end, I suppose I should

have convinced you to love me too.

Sometimes I still hear you, when the wind blows the door open. Sometimes I still see you, when the night sky lights up in stars. Sometimes I still taste you, on a summer's day drinking iced tea. But I know you're not coming back, even if I wish you were still here with me.

While I was losing my breath, running to catch up with you, you were running, breathless, towards someone else.

But I never knew how not to look at you like you were the only woman in the world, just like you never knew how to stop looking away.

What about all those conversations with your

legs draped over mine, my hands in your hair,

the lights dim, breathing in the summer air.

What about all the promises we shared, the

dreams we had, all the things we did right, and

all those moments we made love in the middle

of the night. I've been thinking of all the things

I wanted to say to you, but instead I swallow

them whole. I don't know what happened, I just

know I've lost a piece of my soul.

TARQUIN

And I think about if anyone can hear each piece
of my heart as it tumbles from my chest and
breaks open on the ground. If strangers wonder
why I look so broken, if anyone cares enough to
heal my scars and mend a heart that's bruised
and swollen.

You know it hurts, when you fall asleep in the same clothes you've worn all week, and every radio station is playing your song. The one you shared when you were in love and you thought nothing could change or go wrong. But you also notice the hurt leaving, like when you feel the sun on your face for the first time in months, or you watch your favorite show and you can laugh again, or a stranger's smile seems to ease some of the pain. You know the hurt will eventually heal, if you remind yourself to keep going, to care for yourself a little bit more, than the day before.

TARQUIN

You missed me when you were
out with your friends, drinking at 2AM.
I missed you when I'd see something that
reminded me of you, or in the morning
when I would open my eyes and the view
should have been you.

If I could start over, I would have picked up
every call. I would have stayed up later, just to
remind you how beautiful you are. If I could
start over, I would have opened up more, I
would have shared every thought, embraced
every moment, written down every memory. If
I could start over, I would have told you how
much I loved you every day, every moment,
every second.

When everything was falling apart, it was my
arms you belonged in, but you were halfway
across the country and all the feelings I had
were burning into my skin.

It's breaking me, but you seem happier with him. It's breaking me, because your smile was where the moon and stars begin. It's breaking me but I loved you enough to let you go, I loved you enough to know without me you would grow.

But how could I ever call it closure when the

answer split my heart in two, how could I ever

understand the answer, "I've found someone

new."

On my birthday I wished to never see
you again. Because every time I saw your
name flash across my screen or your
photo somewhere new, somewhere I'd
never been, I felt my heart
break all over again.

You didn't just leave once, you left over and over again. The night we broke up, and the morning after when I realised it wasn't just a dream. You left again when I gave you a box of all your things in my apartment, and you gave me back my sweater you took from my wardrobe. You left when I deleted all our texts, our photos, and again when I finally deleted your number. You left when I couldn't remember your favorite color, when I went to your favorite restaurant, only I'd forgotten we had been there before. You left when I spent Christmas without you, when you weren't my New Year's kiss, when your friend passed me on the street and didn't stop to say hello. You left when I didn't feel the need to tell you about my day, when the world suddenly started carrying on and I realized you had gone, and I was okay.

TARQUIN

Heartbreak tastes like your favorite drink and sounds like your laugh on a Friday night. It smells like the spring we spent hiking the mountains and my t-shirt after you'd worn it all night long. It will always look like your silhouette as you backed out of my driveway and disappeared into the street.

ALL MY
INSECURITIES

It's devasting to constantly question your self worth, to wonder if you deserve to exist on this earth. I'm trying to see the light, instead of crying myself to sleep each night.

It's like my head and my heart are always at war

and I don't know how to get the balance back

anymore.

Everyone always tells me not to be so hard on

myself but the voice inside my head won't let

me go.

Sometimes I think about old memories, won-
dering if I am doing life right. Some days feel
so close yet so far and others a blur. I am over-
whelmed with so many thoughts and what it
means to exist in a world where being yourself is
a daily challenge.

I've just been going around in circles, trying to piece together all my thoughts. Knowing that I am worth more than what I believe I am.

YOU'RE NOT IN LOVE, YOU'RE JUST DRUNK.

I'm drunk and I should call you; but every time

I try to talk about the things that haunt me, I

can't get any of the words to make sense.

Some nights
I feel like the moon
behind the clouds;
will anyone see me enough
to notice all the light
I have .

So many times, I've made excuses, it's too cold,

I'm busy, maybe not tonight. But instead I am

home alone with all these thoughts.

I'm sorry if I let the darkness come between us,

if it was all too much for you. I know I should

have talked more and opened up when you

needed me to.

I am more than the moments I fail, and more
than the days I feel so tired. I know I can fill
myself with good thoughts and things that make
me feel inspired.

These are the things I will try to do...

Be gentle when I am tired.

Be forgiving when I am struggling.

Be loving when I am broken.

Be proud when I am healing.

She was important because she never buried her

pain. She had suffered but refused to be silent.

She was important because she made me feel

brave.

I needed people to remind me of all the reasons I should stay, so if you need reasons, it's that you matter, I'm proud of you, eat something, take deep breaths, take a moment in the sun, remember that you deserve to be here.

I've always been the one that has trouble

admitting how I feel, that bottles everything

inside and never does what I need to heal. But I

will try, I will open up the curtains, take a

shower every day, I will forgive myself and say

the things I want to say.

I'm not going to apologize for taking a moment to breathe or closing my eyes until my heart is calm again. I'm not going to explain my irrational thoughts or why some days it takes every ounce of strength to get out of bed. This is me and I am working every day to love myself the way I was made.

But I have learned to be braver, stronger, bolder.

I have learned to hold onto good things and the

light a little longer. I have learned to breathe,

face my fears, and to stand tall. I have learned

each day won't end like the day before.

It matters that

you are trying

even with small steps.

I don't want the anxiety or the doubt to take
any more moments of happiness. I don't want to
forget my voice or poison the positive thoughts I
have. I want to truly smile, to be excited for the
future, to know that I can do whatever I set my
mind to.

It doesn't matter if you always apologize, even

when there's no need, or if you stutter on how

you feel because you are afraid of what I might

think. It doesn't matter if you need reassurance

or feel too much. I understand, I know you're

trying. I'm trying, too.

The love and forgiveness
I show to others,
I must learn to show
to myself.

Self-care might be a little different depending on who you are – but it's important every day to remind yourself how much your self-care matters.

I've been writing in a journal, every moment I

feel at ease with myself. So, in the moments I

don't think I can go on, I can look back and be

reminded to love myself.

But you have to keep going, all the bad days do
not determine your worth. Each step you take, is
a moment towards growing.

One day I hope to meet the person that takes

notice of my soul and not my faults.

The shadows still creep up on me, begging to

swallow me whole. But instead of perceiving

them as enemies, I will look at them as old

friends, needing a gentle hand to hold until the

morning light returns, just around the bend.

TARQUIN

I am learning that it is okay to want space to grow, that my insecurities need time to heal and my doubt needs to breathe before I can learn to let go.

BUT MOUNTAINS RISE AGAIN, AND RIVERS RETURN TO THE SEA. SO FOR EVERY LONELY NIGHT, I WILL RISE AGAINST THE DOUBT AND SLOWLY FIND A BETTER ME.

ALL MY

DREAMS

You deserve someone who wants to be there in all the messy moments, when things are hard, and life is a struggle. You deserve someone who will ask you what you need instead of guessing. You deserve someone who wants you even when you aren't the easiest choice. You deserve someone who couldn't imagine their life without you.

I've been waiting for someone who is patient,

who doesn't care that I'm a little weird and

quiet, that wants to stay up talking about

important things all through the night.

YOUR MIND IS MAGIC, THE WAY IT
THINKS, HOW RUNNING THROUGH AN
ELECTRIC CURRENT ARE TINY SPARKS
OF YOUR SOUL.

You are allowed to fall in love with your dreams,

to imagine the stars raining down like diamonds

to collect in the night. You are allowed to fall in

love with yourself, after falling apart and then

forgiving your mistakes.

I'm living, I've thrown up from being too drunk, I've failed a test twice, I've lost friends, taken wrong turns and wound up at dead ends. I've had too much junk food, been too shy in front of someone I liked, I've made mistakes but learned from them too; I'm living.

TARQUIN

The smell of ocean water calms me down, how
it reminds me of the feeling of being free. Of
sunlight shining on crystal clear surface, a tide
crashing and tumbling and then finally calm
and still. Of endless possibilities and dreams
unimaginable.

My dreams are filled with starry night conversations, the smell of rain and changing seasons.

She texted me and asked if I wanted to go for a

drive, and I can't tell you how much I smiled.

*She glows
when she is happy.
I just want to make
her happy.*

I'm thinking about you, what it would be to talk about our dream in the early hours of the morning. To wake up and sit on the balcony with cups of coffee, to hold hands, to travel to places we'd never been. To have a love, more beautiful than anyone has ever seen.

Every time my heart beats each pulse reminds

me that I am alive. That my dreams matter, and

my destiny is as sure as the stars align.

We underestimate
how good it feels
to call someone

home.

Her laugh is such a

beautiful sound to me

that I dream of it

at night.

I hope the sun shines brightly for you today. I hope you embrace your dreams and live your life in the best way.

She was free because she held onto her dreams tightly and she never gave up, she never looked away. She was so enchanting I wished she had stayed.

It was about changing my perspective, realizing that sometimes dreams are challenging, and the road is long, but that I would still travel it no matter how long.

One day someone will hold your heart and they will be gentle and kind. You'll be so happy you'll wonder why you almost gave up on love and changing your mind.

I was never the type to daydream, but here I
am, and just getting coffee makes me think of
you

I want someone to explore with,

write letters to, watch scary movies,

ride the subway to far off places,

shop in small markets, watch sunsets,

read poetry and be happy even

when doing absolutely nothing.

You are allowed small moments to stop and

think about the value you hold. Because you do

hold value. You do.

One day I dream of
finding someone
who will want me
forever and not just
for the night.

Let your magic
show and flourish
and grow. You are
too special for no
one to know.

There is something so soft about you, it makes me wonder if we could have long conversations under a starry sky and I wouldn't feel the need to hide my dreams. I wonder if I could break down my walls for you, let you in. Heart to heart and skin to skin.

She was that talk a million miles a minute and

fall into my arms after a long day kind of girl.

The one I thought I would marry but ended up

having to leave her in my dreams.

I search for beauty in everything and by beauty,

I mean what makes you passionate and your

eyes shine. Be who you are and show me your

soul.

The things you think will matter in fifty years, won't. Even if you failed a test or made a mistake or broke your own heart. What will matter are the chances you missed because you hesitated, the souls you passed because you were afraid of being hurt and the moments you list because you were worried what people will say. Live your life now, embrace every second of it.

For what it's worth, I'll never forget her. How she rushed into my life like a comet exploding into a thousand stars. She taught me about myself, about life, about how every moment is only as good as you make it. She told me to hold onto the things you love, and even if I couldn't hold onto her, I'll always hold onto her memory.

TARQUIN

More than anything, more than high hopes and dizzy dreams, more than lazy Sundays, bonfires on the beach, more than long car rides and fireworks, I hope that you find what you are looking for. I hope that the seasons change and bring new flowers, that your dreams shine brighter than the moon, that you always, despite the storms, continue to bloom.

ALL MY
HOPES

I don't know
where I'm going
but I'm going
somewhere.

I can't promise that you won't have days where people upset you or hurt you or make you feel three inches tall. But how you let it affect you changes everything. If you start taking each day as it comes and knowing that your existence is important, eventually the only opinion of you that really matters, is your own.

Things change and
people go,
but better things
are coming.

I pray that you can see your worth, that you

don't lose yourself in times of struggle, that you

understand it's all part of the process.

But for all those who left or decided to unlove

you, this is not a reflection of who you are or

what good things you are capable of.

Some day you will remember these moments and you'll know why things happened the way they did. You'll understand why you had to feel this way. For now, stay strong and keep going.

But I enjoy wishful thinking and mindless dreaming, staring out the window at oceans rolling by and looking up at the clouds and wondering why.

There have been friends who I have lost along the way and it's made my heart ache in the same way lost love has.

Hold onto hope, that beautiful things are on the way. Hold onto it tightly day by day.

TARQUIN

We were so young, but I know each night we hoped the other was the one.

But you need to hold yourself accountable, to keep learning, to acknowledge when you make mistakes, ask questions and always resist conforming.

Remove the people in your life that make you feel inadequate. That aren't interested in the things you love or what makes you happy. They aren't worth your time or your energy.

Life is too short and moves too fast not to tell someone how you feel or forgive when you need to heal. Travel when you can, dance in the rain, fight for what you believe in, wear what you want to wear, sit under the stars, and hope for wonderful things.

Sometimes I think about her and the moments

we shared and even though we're strangers now,

I still hope the best for her.

Every sunrise is a new chance, every day is a new adventure to be unveiled. Don't let heartache take away opportunities that are yet to set sail.

There will be plenty of moments and I won't know what to say but I'll always be there for you, you'll always be able to talk to me and know that in my heart is a safe space, a place to rest your hopes and your fears.

When I finally accepted that
I couldn't please everyone I
began to hope for myself.

One of these days you won't feel so broken and

all the things that you hoped for, will find you.

I promise someone is out there who won't look

at all your baggage and think it's too much to

carry. Someone who wants to unpack

conversations and be open with their thoughts.

Someone who loves you just as you are.

Someone who will grow with you through every

hurdle and never think you are a burden.

It felt like the end of the world, like I had lost everything and all hope. And I know we hurt each other, and one blamed the other. I know things were messy and the long lonely nights became too hard. But I want you to know even after everything I loved you and I'll always love you. I'll always want happiness to find both of us.

While the shadows tell you that you are broken,

I hope the sun reminds you that you are

beautiful, the flowers remind you to bloom every

season and you hold onto the belief that every-

thing happens for a reason.

Even after all the times I've been hurt, I'm still standing, still hopeful, still breathing.

She was a risk _I_ wanted to take, an adventure _I_ wanted forever, a journey worth exploring, _I_ still dream of her when the sky turns soft.

I hope you never become afraid
to love me, that you always find
sanctuary in my heart.

'Remember that hope exists within you. It lives in every moment you make it through.

ALL MY

LOVE

You dared me and I'm
so glad I had the
nerve to love you.

I just want to know everything about you, learn

all there is to learn, to be able to call you home.

Are you thinking of me, too, because its been

almost all night and my mind is on you.

I'll always remember those moments we spent
driving around the neighborhood listening to
our favorite songs, my hand on your thigh, and
your smile lighting up the night.

It's not always about wanting her, it's about appreciating her, valuing her, listening to her soul.

Will you love me in the years to come, as you do right now?

Always in my arms
you belong
the only soul
I'll ever call home.

Since knowing her
my heart beats in a way
it has never beat before.

I just want to memorize you like my favorite

lyrics and my favorite movie. I want to mem-

orize every curve, every line, every dimple on

your body. I want to memorize every laugh,

every touch, every detail of you that means so

much.

It's the way you look at me even if we aren't

doing anything in particular, you look at me as

though I am worth something, as though

together we can move mountains.

When I am thinking about you, the world splits open into bright colors. You are the sun on a dull day, the stars that light up the night sky, the view of the ocean as we're passing by.

You smile and I melt, almost fall to pieces for

the way I feel about you. There is a softness to

the way you say my name, like it's the only name

you know. I think the universe brought us

together, I just hope you'll say my name forever.

The cure for love sickness
is kindness, hot chocolate
and soft colors.

You are allowed to be on your own, to love your-
self and hold your own hand. You will someday
know what it means to grow within yourself, to
understand your demons and how to combat
them. You will create your own dreams and
goals and be the person standing in your own
corner. Someday you will look back and wonder
why you weren't always your own hero.

It took me so long to realize that sometimes the best kind of love, is falling in love with simply existing.

We don't all have the privilege to leave

everything behind and travel to find ourselves.

So if you find yourself stuck and in a situation

that seems impossible, just remember your life

starts and ends with you, it belongs to you and

no one can take that away.

She was the kind of girl that always had sunflowers on her windowsill, the kind of girl that spoke about the world as though she had lived for centuries, the kind that had words for things I had never even heard of. She was the kind of girl that turned heads but never knew, the kind of girl that was always honest, always true, always moving through seasons hoping for new adventures. She was the kind of girl that never made me look back.

Kiss her so that you both see stars swimming in your eyes. Kiss her, so the ocean shudders and the sky erupts in color.

Be vulnerable, talk about the things that hurt,

and the moments that chipped away at your

soul. Talking lets the light back in, lets the heart

beat again.

You can call me at 4am when you're sad or lonely or just want to hear my voice. You can wake me up, I'll probably already be dreaming of you. I just want to be here for you, let you know you're wanted even when your shoulders feel a little heavy, even when the world feels too big and you aren't ready.

You're the person I want to
stay up all night talking to.

The person who believes in me
and everything I do.

She fills me to the brim with possibility, endless

laughter, pounding pulses, she is my

happily ever after.

It will feel simple and easy. Like you have done this for a thousand lifetimes. It's because that's your person and you'll never question the love. Even in the times of struggle it will still feel simple. It will still feel as though everything makes sense.

Even if she's still finding her way and going

through the motions of every day, I still love her,

I still love that we can discover life together.

Some of the best moments haven't even

happened yet, but I can't wait to spend them all

with you.

Meeting you was like finding

a new home and knowing

I'll always be safe.

I am in love with a beautiful sunset and how it reminds me of you. If you ever need to kiss me, talk to me, hold me near, you can find me here.

Thank you

Tarquin
xx

follow along on instagram
@tarquinpoetry

ISBN: 9781703345889

Made in the USA
Las Vegas, NV
25 March 2021

20120697R00115